Christian Rhyme Poems

Inspiring For The Soul

By

Jerrel C. Thomas

Christian Rhyme Poems

Inspiring For The Soul

Copyright © 2015 Jerrel C. Thomas

All rights reserved.

ISBN-13: 978-1514300336

ISBN-10: 1514300338

Books By Jerrel C. Thomas

The Comforter

My Memories, From The End Of The Road

Peanut The Mouse, And Friends

Christian Rhyme Poems

The Missing Words

There's Nothing Like Good Home Cooking

Understanding The God Of The Bible

Information

To find out more information about Jerrel C. Thomas, and about Brother William Marrion Branham, then please go to these websites:

Books By Jerrel C. Thomas

https://jerrelcthomas.wixsite.com/my-site-4

Voice Of God Recordings

http://branham.org/

The Message

http://themessage.com/

Dedication

I would like to dedicate this book to my nephew Gaylan Ralph Thomas II - nicknamed Cricket

Number of Poems

Introduction

I have always had a heart for poetry, poems, and rhyming. I decided to publish my rhyming pomes in this book for you.

Back when I was just a little boy, my mother read to me one of her poems. I thought it was one of the greatest things I've ever heard. I wished I could remember the words, but I was so little then and can't remember. But I honestly believe that it was her poem that got me to write my own.

I hope this book will be a blessing, insomuch that you can gain strength for each new day. Enjoy!

A Spiritual Quote

There's only one way that you'll ever be able to receive this wonderful Comforter is when you believe on the Lord Jesus Christ, confess your sins, repent, have Christian baptism administered to you, and a promise that God will fill you with the Holy Spirit. That's His promise. He cannot go back on That. It's His promise. I've always said, if a person was thoroughly taught, and was repented, and from their heart had believed on God with all that was within them, and when they are baptized, immediately the Holy Spirit will come upon them, because He promised to do so. He promised it. "You shall receive the Holy Ghost, for the promise is unto you."

Quote From:

60-0301 - He Careth For You

Rev. William Marrion Branham

http://www.branham.org/

1 - In The Shadow Of The Night

All the clouds are gray, and the sky is dark as night. Soft words are spoken, and there's a twinkle, of a flicker of light.

The presence of a Man walks by, and Mighty and Powerful is He.

Kneeling to pray, He says a prayer for me.

The sky becomes brighter, and the leaves of the trees turn green.

The flowers begin to bloom, and there's a warm gentle breeze.

Thank you, Lord, for setting me free...

2 - Lonely And Despair

Where are you going? You look so scared.

You won't turn around, and there's darkness everywhere.

Traveling you must go, traveling in despair.

Trying to look up, but never looking there.

There's a spark of a little smile, but it turns into a frown.

You stretch out your hand and listening for a sound.

Desperately searching, for someone who is sweet and kind.

The roadmap says go this way, but I pay it no mind.

You feel a touch from someone, and you feel so helpless and blind.

Your eyes began to open, and you find yourself lost in time.

It seems like it will never end, and the sun begins to shine.

You finally turned to see who it is, and it's someone you had on your mind.

Oh Lord Jesus… You're grace and mercy, you were there all the time.

3 - It's A Rainy Night In My Soul

The rain keeps on coming, deep within my soul.

I'd like to throw in the towel, but I just can't let it go.

I can't help it; it comes from deep within.

My heart used to be soft, but now it like tin.

I tried to find a way of escape, but I don't know where to begin.

I cried out to Jesus and repented of all my sins.

The window now is shut, and the rain is no longer coming in.

A new window is now open, and now my new life begins. All my bad habits seem to fade away.

I'm striving for a new life, and I found a new life today.

I'm no longer blind, and may I say, no more rainy nights, and the clouds fade away.

4 - Believe In Jesus

The birds are singing so freely, and time slips away.

I find myself lost, in a wagon full of hay.

The wagon flows so softly, over yellow fields.

The horses are so gentle, as they clicked up their heels.

The Master turns and looks at me, and then He begins to speak.

His Words are so gentle, but with power that is so unique.

"Life isn't worth living, unless you believe in Me…"

5 - The Snow Flake

Way up high, up in the blue sky.

Clouds are forming, and a little snowflake blinks his eye.

Life is so easy; he just floats in the breeze.

He finds himself sleeping, sleeping with ease.

Way up in the sky, time seems to pass by.

He finds himself melting, changes his disguise.

Now he's a water droplet, and he twinkles as he passes by, he's all new, the change made him cry.

He hits the ground and disappears; but not for long, he's raptured and reappears.

So go on living your life and do the best you can.

Give your life to Christ, and He'll give you a helping hand.

One day we must all die. But remember we'll be resurrected again; and we'll never leave his side.

6 - Lonely Girl

Hey there lonely girl, don't be afraid.

Please give me your hand, you know there's a better way.

Walk with Me and talk with Me, and the sun will shine again. Sometimes we wander off, and sometimes we sin.

Though sometimes life can hurt, and it seems like it repeats. But in time things will all mend, and you will be complete.

But put your trust in Me, and My love will flow. You're like beautiful flower, and you'll begin to grow.

Tomorrow is a better day. Full of laughter along the way. Keep on walking in the light, and your night will turn today.

Come along with Me lonely girl, and don't be afraid.

Let me wipe your teardrops, and I'll make them go away.

I'll be your friend, no matter what people say.

Just look to Me and pray.

I'll bring you happiness through thick and thin.

My name is Jesus, and I'll be with you and till the very end…

7 - Creation

The birds, the trees, everything you see; God even gave life to you and me.

The day lily, and the roses, and the golden dandelion; everything may be struggling, but life keeps trying.

The grass, and even the weeds; they all have a purpose for you and me. The stream, the rivers, the lakes, and oceans, oh a sight to see.

Why did God make all these things? Because he cares. He made them all, just for you and me.

8 - A Teardrop

Oh no, it happened again.

Why does life even go on, will it ever end?

Nothing seems to turn out right, and things always go wrong.

It's all like, a sad song.

A teardrop running down my face.

And here comes another one, trying to keep pace.

My emotions are overwhelming, and my thoughts go back in time.

Here comes another tear, not too far behind.

Like rain drops, they keep falling, falling from my eyes.

I look up to heaven, and I began to pray, and I ask why?

Is there any hope for little ol' me? Then I hear a soft and gentle voice, a voice from up above.

I felt His hand, a gentle touch of a love.

A little mercy and grace, and a little key.

"Unlock the door, and you will find Me."

"Fear not my child, for today I set you free.

I give you love, and life for eternity ..."

9 - The Missing Piece

There's a piece of me missing, and I search diligently.

A piece of my life, a piece that was meant to be.

All the leaves are brown, and the grass is no longer green.

The sky is gray, and there's a little chill in the breeze.

This piece that I'm missing, is something I must find.

I must look everywhere, but I don't have much time.

Everything is so dark, and shadows at every turn.

Looking in every crevice, there's so much for me to learn.

Will I find what I'm looking for, or will life come to an end?

I must find what I'm looking for, it's almost like a lost friend.

But there's a higher place, yes, I must look and see.

This may be what I'm looking for, this might be the place for me.

I climb over rocks and debris, hoping to find something that'll set me free.

As I look up into heaven, I see a light shining down through the trees.

This is what I was looking for; but you know it found me.

I don't know how to explain it, but His Words spoke to me.

When I embraced it, I was set free.

All I had to do was repent and be baptize.

The peace that I was missing, became a part of me. Now life is so simple, and now I am set free.

Now I'm no longer wandering in darkness, but now I see the light.

I found my missing piece. Now I will praise the Lord all my life.

10 - His Treasure

What's that I hear, falling on my ear?

Its love that passes all understanding and overcoming all fear.

Walking alone, I immediately feel His presence.

What does He want with me, me an old peasant?

Rags for my garments, and no shoes on my feet.

I'm so insignificant, why would he have anything to do with me?

He reaches out His hand, but I'm so ashamed to go near.

"Come here my child, you have nothing to fear."

I began to walk, trembling as I go.

Not knowing what to expect, but this I know.

His love radiates all around me, from my head to my toes. There is joy everywhere, and joy for my woes.

Before I could speak, he grants me my wish.

Help for the hopeless, and food in my dish.

He wants to meet your needs too.

Don't be shy, He's waiting for you…

11 - I Wonder?

I wonder if, he forgot about me.

I wonder, why he just doesn't see.

I wonder, if he even remembers my grace.

I wonder, is he's still running in the race.

I wonder, if he understands.

I wonder, if he remembers my pierced feet and hands.

I wonder, why he doesn't pray.

I wonder, is this you today?

12 - Where I First Began

The pride in me, is just a man.

The clouds fade away, as I walk through the sand.

The water rushes in and covers my feet.

What must I do, to overcome my defeat?

I once walked with Jesus, long ago.

But I walked away, from to and fro.

I stopped in my tracks and began to think.

What's wrong with me, there's a missing link.

I must get back together and be strong once again.

I repent to you Jesus, for all my sin.

Now my pride is gone, and humility set in.

Thank you, Jesus, for giving me hope, and letting me back in, where I first began.

13 - I Knew You When

I knew you when, before time began.

I knew you when, you first became my friend.

I knew you when, you were lonely.

I knew you when, you were only…

I knew you when, you were the one.

I knew you when, you became my son.

I knew you when, you fell away.

I knew you when, and may I say?

I knew you when, I brought you back in.

I knew you when, I took away all your sin.

I knew you when, I knew you when, I knew you when…

14 - When I Thought All Hope Was Gone

I'm so exhausted, I can't continue anymore.
I'm weak and tired, and my body so sore.

I keep struggling, even though I can't go on.
I know there's hope, but it's been so long.
What's that?

I see someone moving, it's coming my way.
His presence, almighty, and strong.

I feel weak, unsteady, and like a piece of clay.

A Sunbeam shoots from His presence, lands upon me.

He begins to walk toward me, and He has something to say:

"Come to me, you who are weak and heavy laden, and I will set you free."

When I thought all hope was gone, he made a way for me.

15 - Being Thankful

It was the night before Christmas, as I lay down on my bed.

The door begins to open, and my mommy takes a peek, and she said:

"Sandy, you get some sleep now, and don't forget to pray…"

"Now I lay me down to sleep, I pray to the Lord my soul to keep.

Bless mommy and daddy, and all my relatives too.

Leave not one out, whenever You do.

I know I'm too little, and You're so strong.

You're the one that can help me, whenever things are going wrong.

And thank You for giving me, Your special gift.

When I'm down and out, Jesus gives me a lift.

Even though I can't walk, mommy hast to carry me around.

I won't give up, and I will never frown.

So, all I ask for Christmas, is that You keep mommy and daddy safe.

Thank you, and good night, it's getting late.

Merry Christmas... May I say, this is the best Christmas, on this Christmas Eve Day."

16 - The Blue Forget Me Not

Sitting in my rocking chair, outside on my porch.

The sun is setting, and it's all bright red like a torch.

Only God can paint the sky like this.

Just rocking away in my rocking chair, where I sit.

My husband is no longer with me, but I know he's close by.

He's with my Lord, way, way up there in the sky.

I reach in my pocket, and there I find. A little yellow paper, as if it was trying to hide.

With anticipation I opened it to read, and to my surprise, there was a little seed, and then I began to read.

When you find this yellow paper, my dear. I want you to lend me your ear.

I would like you to take this little seed, and I would like you to plant it for me.

And when the flower begins to grow, it will remind you of me.

Just a little Forget Me Not, just a little seed.
I know the Lord is with you; he took all your sin away.

And one of these days you'll be with me. but for now, remember me, with this Forget Me Not flower seed I pray.

17 - The Lemonade Stand

It was a bright warm sunny day when my brother and I when out to play.

Mother was making a fresh batch of lemonade, and it wasn't long, and I heard my mother say:

"Come on you two, I have something I would like you to do."

So, we ran inside and shut the door, we tried to stop but we slid on the floor.

Mom looked at us and shook her head. Then she turned around, and then she said: "

"I have some lemonade, and your lemonade stand. Would you like to sell some lemonade, I'll give you a helping hand?"

My brother and I looked at each other, and then our heads went up and down.

It was a quiet day that day, a quiet day all over town.

She helped us set up the lemonade stand, and when she looked up there stood a man.

The old man had old, ragged clothing, and holes in his knees, and on the side of his pants, a key ring full of keys.

"Would you like some lemonade?" I was asking the man.

He then looked up, and stretched out his hand…

"I'm sorry I have no money." With a sad look on his face.

"That's OK you can have this one for free." As I bent over to tie my shoelace.

Mom looked at him and smiled. Then she handed him a cup of lemonade.

He took the cup, and he began to drink. As he started to walk away, and I began to think.

I feel so good inside, knowing I helped someone today.

But when he turned and looked at me, I saw a glimpse of Jesus, and then He faded away…

18 - Elizabeth

I've always wanted to accomplish something in my life.

I've always loved sunshine, but sometimes it's dark as night.

I've always needed to be doing something, but I come up short, at the end of the day.

Why is it that things just don't work out for me? Oh well, what can I say?

A nice cup of coffee, and a friend to talk to; it makes life just a little easier, and not so blue.

But there's one thing in my life, that I can count on each day.

He's always there with me, and somehow, He shows me the way. Thank you, Jesus!

19 - Always

I've always got sunshine, even on cloudy days.

When I pray to Jesus, He always makes a way.

20 - Moments

Sometimes in moments like these, I sing unto Jesus with ease.

The yellow flowers, and the leaves on the trees, and look there's a butterfly in the breeze.

In moments like these, I dance and shout the victory.

The grass is so brilliant and green, and the air is so crisp and clean.

I love the Lord, more than I can say. Moments with Him, always bright up my day…

21 - Little Bee

Busy, busy little bee; flying by me in the breeze.

She whirls around and around, and then she come back towards me.

Busy, busy little bee; landing on a flower, right next to me.

Gathering balls of pollen on her hind legs, a little nectar as she goes on her way.

Life is so simple, and life is so free.

Busy, busy little bee; making honey for you and me.

God's little blessing, in a little busy bee.

22 - The Cross

As I walk up the hill, and the crowd was so still.

Not knowing what to expect, as I got a little closer, I began to kneel.

Looking up, I see this man.

His arms are stretched out on a cross, and there's nails in his hands.

There're nails in his feet, and blood streaming down.

People were crying beside me, and then I began to frown.

I then hear Him say: "Verily I say unto thee, today thou be with me in paradise."

I then ask a question. "Who is this man, and what is his name?"

A Roman soldier turned and looked at me. "They say he's the king of the Jews, and his name is Jesus. What is it to you?"

I looked at him, but I had nothing to say.

I've heard about Jesus, and that he was to die for me one day.

I felt something come over me, and Jesus filled me within.

So, I accepted Him that day, asking Him to take all my sin.

And from that day on, He has never parted; for

He became a part of me, and a place in my heart…

23 - Why Me?

I'll never understand, what Jesus sees in me.

I'm always looking to Him, and He always sets me free.

I never do anything right, and I'm always in the wrong.

Not that I mean to, but it seems like my days are long gone.

Sometimes I wonder, is there really any hope for me?

But then I'm reminded, He died on the cross to set me free. So now I know, why me.

24 - Don't Give Up

Where are you going, don't give up?

Always push forward, are you doing enough?

There's always hope, just look to Him up above.

He will shine on you, His wonderful love...

25 - A New Day

There's a chill in the air, and frost on the ground.

I once had a smile, but now I have a frown.

Life was so simple, but now I'm having a hard time.

Climbing up this mountain, and trying to find...

There's hope and forgiveness, just be on the blue.

There's a Man called Jesus, a friend that's always true.

I prayed a prayer, and I heard from above.

A warm breeze shot over me, and I felt His love.

The frost on the ground began to melt, and help was on the way.

He set me free and gave me a new day.

26 - Believe Within

As you looked out your window, you see a butterfly in the breeze. You see a robin up in a tree and singing so freely.

The grass is so bright and green, and the sky is bright and blue. If you're down in the dumps, and you can't get up, there is a way out for you.

Just look to the Creator, and you will find a friend. Just ask and ye will receive. All you must do is believe within...

27 - My Friend And I

My friend is now long gone, He has gone away.

The times we shared will always be, and may I say?

We used to walk along this sandy beach, and we would stop and pray. Time will not always be here, and time will slip away.

Those moments are still in my mind, and they'll be there for a long, long time.

And if it takes 1000 summers, walking along the shores.

I will walk, by the sea, for that open door.

But until my life is done, I'll hold onto the memories.

Jesus gave me hope, and the sun will shine through the evergreens.

There's life beyond this earthly life because my friend Jesus gave His life for mine.

One day my friend and I, will live together. Life that will last for ever and ever; and that a long, long time.

28 - The Lust Of My Flesh

Sin is all around me, the lust of my flesh is strong.

I know help is on the way, but why is it taking so long?

I'll do the best I can, and that's just about all I can do.

It makes me wonder, is there really any hope for me and you?

I've got to start thinking positive, that's what it takes to get through.

Nothing is hopeless, when I believe in You.

It's You dear Lord Jesus, that makes my spirt brand new. The lust of my flesh will die, but

it's only your Holy Spirit that will keep me renewed.

So, I will never give up, no matter how many times I fall.

You will always be there for me and deliver me of them all.

In loving memory of Ethan R. Stoner

May 26, 1966 - July 8, 2015

29 - Visitors Of Room 17

My friend is in the hospital, and he's not expecting to live.

My friends and I are going out to see him, and we're all sad within.

Hope seems to be all gone; all we can do is pray.

But if it's his time to go, not even prayer will stand in his way.

We all drive up to the hospital, and we all get out and walk in.

When we found his room number 17, I'm wondering is this really the end?

When he sees me, he reaches out and gives me a hug.

There's a little smile on his face, and lots of love.

A sister in the Lord, ask if I would sing for him a song.

At first, I hesitate, but that didn't last too long.

I started singing: "I'll Never Let Go Of Your Hand"

I see he was enjoying it. I reached out and grabbed his hand.

Then I began to tremble, and with a little quiver in my song.

I could see he was suffering, and the night was long.

The pain and anguish that he was going through, but he tried to put it all aside.

As we all stood around him... I began to cry.

We stayed there quite a while, but then it was time for us to leave.

It seemed like hope was all gone, but I just had to believe.

He made his life right, with the Master long ago.

And the love of Jesus, made it so…

Two days later he passed away, and now he's up above.

But I know he loved the visitors of room 17, who came with lots of Love…

30 - The Word

God's Words of healing, it's all there for me.

When I read His Word, it becomes a part of me.

His Word is His Spirit, and His Spirit lives in me.

Because I'm a part of Him, He's a part of me.

The more I read His Word, and the Message He had for me.

The more He filled me with His Spirit, which He gives so freely.

So read all you can and be filled with His Word.

He will seal you until the day of redemption, and with wisdom that's been unheard.

Made in the USA
Middletown, DE
13 May 2023

30542447R00033